DATE DUE

Cultural Traditions in
Thailand

Molly
Aloian

Crabtree Publishing Company
www.crabtreebooks.com

Crabtree Publishing Company

www.crabtreebooks.com

Author: Molly Aloian
Publishing plan research and development:
 Sean Charlebois, Reagan Miller
 Crabtree Publishing Company
Project coordinator: Kathy Middleton
Editors: Adrianna Morganelli, Crystal Sikkens
Photo research: Crystal Sikkens
Design: Margaret Amy Salter
Production coordinator: Margaret Amy Salter
Prepress technician: Margaret Amy Salter
Print coordinator: Katherine Berti

Cover: Temples in Chiang Mai, Thailand (background);
Firework Festival in Chiangmai, Thailand (top); Thai
performers (middle center); orchids (middle left and right);
Buddha statue (bottom left); boat with fruit at floating
market (bottom right); Tom Yam Koong and Squid soup
with noodles (bottom middle)

Title page: Dancers perform a traditional Thai dance at the
Phimai Light and Sound Festival at Phimai Stone Castle,
Thailand.

Photographs:
Associated Press: Apichart Weerawong: page 15
Dreamstime: Just2shutter: page 9 (inset); Namatae: pages
 22–23; Christian Baumle: page 25
Shutterstock: cover (except middle center and bottom right),
 pages 4, 6, 10, 14, 16, 18 (top), 29 (bottom), 30 (bottom), 31;
 Alexander Gitlits: cover (middle center); Poznyakov: cover
 (bottom right); Worakit Sirijinda: title page; Charlie
 Edward: page 5; Dmitry Berkut: page 7; 1000 Words: page
 8 (inset); GOLFX: pages 8–9 (background); Yuttasak
 Jannarong: page 12; axel2001: page 13 (top);
 topten22photo: page 13 (bottom); Satin: pages 17, 18
 (bottom); Keepsmiling4u: page 21; 501room: page 26;
 OlegD: page 27 (left); chantal de bruijne: page 27 (right);
 Thor Jorgen Udvang: page 28; Sam DCruz: page 29 (top)
Wikimedia Commons: Sry85: page 11; Xiengyod: page 19;
Sacca: page 20; Xiengyod: page 24; Aristitleism: page 30 (top)

Library and Archives Canada Cataloguing in Publication

Aloian, Molly
 Cultural traditions in Thailand / Molly Aloian.

(Cultural traditions in my world)
Includes index.
Issued also in electronic format.
ISBN 978-0-7787-7519-5 (bound).--ISBN 978-0-7787-7524-9 (pbk.)

 1. Festivals--Thailand--Juvenile literature. 2. Thailand--Social
life and customs--Juvenile literature. I. Title. II. Series: Cultural
traditions in my world

GT4878.A2A46 2012   j394.269593   C2012-904359-1

Library of Congress Cataloging-in-Publication Data

Aloian, Molly.
 Cultural traditions in Thailand / Molly Aloian.
 p. cm. -- (Cultural traditions in my world)
 Includes index.
 ISBN 978-0-7787-7519-5 (reinforced library binding) -- ISBN 978-0-7787-7524-9
(pbk.) -- ISBN 978-1-4271-9043-7 (electronic pdf) -- ISBN 978-1-4271-9097-0
(electronic html)
 1. Holidays--Thailand--Juvenile literature. 2. Festivals--Thailand--Juvenile
literature. 3. Thailand--Social life and customs--Juvenile literature. I. Title.
II. Series: Cultural traditions in my world.

 GT4878.A2A47 2013
 394.269593--dc23

                    2012024787

Crabtree Publishing Company

www.crabtreebooks.com   1-800-387-7650

Printed in Canada/102013/MA20130906

Published in Canada
Crabtree Publishing
616 Welland Ave.
St. Catharines, ON
L2M 5V6

Published in the United States
Crabtree Publishing
PMB 59051
350 Fifth Avenue, 59th Floor
New York, New York 10118

Published in the United Kingdom
Crabtree Publishing
Maritime House
Basin Road North, Hove
BN41 1WR

Published in Australia
Crabtree Publishing
3 Charles Street
Coburg North
VIC 3058

Contents

About Thailand

Thailand is a country in Southeast Asia. It is a country of many different cultures, and people celebrate different cultural traditions. Cultural traditions are holidays, festivals, special days, and customs celebrated each year. Most of the people in Thailand follow the religion of Buddhism, which was founded by a teacher called the Buddha. People, called Buddhists, follow his teachings and honor ancient Buddhist traditions.

Bangkok is the capital of Thailand.

Some people in Thailand are Chinese-Thai. They celebrate many Chinese holidays, such as Chinese New Year. Malay people live mainly in the southern part of Thailand. They celebrate Muslim holidays. Groups of hill people from the north have different cultural traditions. They worship **ancestors**.

The dragon dance is a popular part of this Chinese New Year festival in Bangkok.

Let's Celebrate!

People in Thailand celebrate weddings, birthdays, christenings, and other important days throughout the year. During many Thai weddings, both the bride and groom wear a crown of looped white yarn called a mongkol. The two mongkols are joined together with a string, which is a **symbol** of the union between husband and wife.

Part of a traditional Thai wedding involves a blessing where the couple places their hands on pillows and a string is tied around their wrists. This is suppose to bring them happiness and healthy children.

Did You Know?
Children from Buddhist families often wear charms on their arms or legs. Charms are objects that people believe will protect them or bring good luck.

Children are an important part of the country. Every January they celebrate a holiday called Children's Day. On Children's Day, parents take their children out to have fun. There are often special events and certain museums and amusement parks that let children in for free or for half price.

These children are having fun on an elephant on Children's Day in the city of Ko Chang.

Magha Puja

Many holidays and festivals in Thailand celebrate special events in the life of the Buddha. Magha Puja is an important Buddhist celebration that usually takes place in the last week of February or in early March. On this day, people remember the great events that took place during the Buddha's lifetime. They honor the Buddha and his teachings.

Buddhists visit temples to say prayers on Magha Puja.

8

On Magha Puja, Buddhists gather at sunset in temples to participate in candlelight **processions**. They walk around a **shrine** or an image of the Buddha three times. They try to avoid committing any **sins** and try to **purify** their minds.

Did You Know?
During Magha Puja, Thai people give **monks** food. It is believed that the Thai people will gain **merit** by giving food to the monks.

Chakri Day

People celebrate Chakri Day on April 6 to **commemorate** the founding of the Chakri **dynasty** and the many contributions of the kings. The Chakri dynasty has been ruling Thailand since 1782. On Chakri Day, the people of Thailand express their love and loyalty to their current king, Bhumibol Adulyadej, also known as King Rama IX, as well as past kings.

The Grand Palace in the city of Bangkok was built by King Rama I, the founder of the Chakri dynasty. On Chakri Day, the current king visits the Grand Palace to honor King Rama I and other past kings.

The current king of Thailand performs a royal ceremony on Chakri Day to pay respect to his ancestors. During the ceremony, he lays a wreath at King Rama I's statue in the Grand Palace. Banks, schools, and government offices close for the holiday, but most other businesses are open. The national flag is proudly displayed and people light incense and lay wreaths of flowers and garlands before statues of King Rama I.

Did You Know?
King Rama I was a famous military leader. He came to the throne during the country's war with a neighboring country called Burma. Afterward, he moved the capital city of the country to Krung Thep, which is known today as Bangkok.

This statue of King Rama I is located at The Memorial Bridge in Bangkok, Thailand.

Songkran

The Songkran festival is the traditional New Year's celebration in Thailand. Songkran begins on April 13 and ends on April 15. It is one of three New Year's Day holidays in Thailand. People also celebrate New Year's Day on January 1 and Chinese New Year in February.

Did You Know?
On the night before the beginning of Songkran, many people clean their homes and get rid of any items they do not need.

During Songkran, people take the time to pay respect to elders. They often give flowers and garlands to older family members, friends, and neighbors.

Songkran is also an ancient water festival. Some people celebrate by throwing water on one another! They walk the streets with containers of water or water guns and drench each other and those that pass by. It is believed that doing so will wash away bad luck and bring good luck in the year to come.

Painting elephants is a popular tradition during Songkran. Even the elephants get into the spirit of the water festival by spraying people.

Labor Day

People celebrate Labor Day on May 1. They recognize the importance of Thai labor workers and honor their contributions to the country. The day is about showing gratitude to the working citizens of Thailand. There are song and dance performances and people listen to speeches about Thailand and its history in the Royal Plaza in Bangkok. People watch Labor Day parades and attend special remembrance ceremonies.

This farmworker is planting rice. Rice is planted by hand in flooded fields.

Almost half of all workers in Thailand work in **agriculture**. Rice is the country's most important crop. Thailand sells more rice around the world than any other country. Labor Day is also a holiday celebrated by many other countries. It is believed that labor day celebrations developed from ancient customs celebrating spring.

Did You Know?
In 1993, a fire at a toy factory near Bangkok killed over 180 workers and injured more than 500. It was one of the world's worst industrial fires. On Labor Day, people in Thailand remember those who died or were injured in the fire and work to make working conditions safe for everyone.

Buddha's Birthday

People celebrate Visakha Puja or Buddha's Birthday in April or May. It commemorates the birth, **enlightenment**, and death of the Buddha, which all happened on the same month and day. People gather together at temples before dawn to attend special ceremonies, sing **hymns**, and bring offerings of flowers, candles, and other items.

Temples, such as this one in Ayutthaya, are decorated with lights, candles, and lanterns on Visakha Puja.

Parades take place throughout Thailand to show honor and respect to the Buddha on Visakha Puja.

On Buddha's Birthday, many people also try to bring happiness to sick, old, or injured people. At school, children celebrate the day with activities that promote understanding and compassion for others.

Did You Know?
The Buddha was born in southern Nepal, in India, at the foot of the Himalaya Mountains.

Royal Plowing Ceremony

The Royal Plowing Ceremony is an ancient ceremony that marks the beginning of the rice-growing season in Thailand. Rice is an important source of food in Thailand. There is no fixed date for the ceremony, but it is usually held in May, June, or July.

Did You Know?
Thailand is one of the world's largest rice producers.

In recent years, the Royal Plowing Ceremony has taken place at Sanam Luang, which is an open field and public square in front of the Grand Palace in Bangkok.

In the ceremony, two **sacred** oxen are hitched to a wooden plow. They plow a long groove in the ground, and rice seeds are thrown in the dirt. After the plowing, the oxen are offered water and plates of food including rice, corn, green beans, and grass. People believe the food the oxen choose to eat predicts how good the harvest will be.

People search for the rice seeds after the Royal Plowing Ceremony because they believe the seeds are lucky.

Dharma Day

Dharma Day or Asalha Puja marks the very beginning of the Buddha's teaching and the start of the Buddhist religion. It is a day to express gratitude to the Buddha and other teachers of Buddhism for sharing their knowledge.

This painting depicts the first teachings of the Buddha.

Many Thai people meditate on Dharma Day. Buddhists meditate to reflect or think carefully and quietly about the Buddha's teachings.

People usually celebrate Dharma Day in June or July with readings from Buddhist **scriptures**. They also take extra time to think about the meanings of the scriptures. Many people go to a temple to celebrate with monks or nuns. Nuns are females that follow the same rules as monks.

Did You Know?
Monks are highly respected in Thailand. They do not own anything, but depend on the people of their community for food and essential items. They offer blessings to the Thai people and teachings from the scriptures.

Khao Phansa

In July, Khao Phansa marks the beginning of the period of **retreat** for Buddhist monks, which lasts until October. Monks are not allowed to leave their temples. It is a time to meditate and study Buddhist scriptures. During Khao Phansa, Thai men and boys are often **ordained** and become monks.

Did You Know?
Khao Phansa takes place during Thailand's rainy season when the rice crops are grown. Originally, monks were required to remain in one temple during Lent so they would not step on crops as they traveled.

Khao Phansa is also known as the Candle Festival. In the days leading up to the festival, people make huge candles out of beeswax. The candles can be up to 6.6 feet (two meters) tall and are carved with patterns and designs. On the day of the festival, the candles are paraded around towns and cities on special floats. The parades end at temples and the candles are presented to the newly ordained monks.

This large beeswax candle float features a number of dragons in various sizes.

The Queen's Birthday

The Queen's Birthday is a public holiday in Thailand. On August 12, people decorate streets and buildings with colorful lights, flowers, flags, and portraits of Queen Sirikit, the current queen of Thailand. It is a day to celebrate the birth of the queen and remember everything she has done for the people of Thailand.

Did You Know?
Queen Sirikit was born Mom Rajawongse Sirikit Kitiyakara on August 12, 1932.

Queen Sirikit has been honorary president of the Thai Red Cross since 1956. This role allowed her to help the Thai people recover from the tsunami disaster in southern Thailand in 2004. She is also known for assisting the many refugees from Cambodia and Burma who live in Thailand.

Members of the Thai army march in a parade for Queen Sirikit's birthday ceremony.

This dance group is performing for Queen Sirikit's birthday, which is also celebrated nationwide as Mother's Day.

Loy Krathong

Loy Krathong is one of the most beautiful Thai celebrations. It is held on the evening of the full moon in November, following the rice harvest. Thai people give thanks to the water spirits for the water they provided during the growing season.

Thai dancers and colorful floats are paraded through the streets during the opening ceremonies of the Loy Krathong festival.

During the night of the celebration, people gather beside canals, rivers, and other waterways. They place candles, food, flowers, coins, and other items in krathongs that are set in the waterways to float away. Government offices, corporations, and other large organizations usually make huge, decorated, raft-like krathongs that are often judged in contests.

Did You Know?
In Thai, the word "Loy" means "to float." A "krathong" is a circular, floating object. A krathong can be made out of anything from banana leaves to bread to Styrofoam.

The waterways in Thailand glow with light from the moon and the thousands of candles and lanterns that are set afloat on Loy Krathong.

The King's Birthday

On December 5, people celebrate the birthday of His Majesty King Bhumibol Adulyadej, the world's longest reigning monarch. On this day, people in Thailand and Thai people living throughout the world, show their love and **reverence** to the king. They pay respect to the king and show gratitude for all he has done for Thailand.

Did You Know?
The golden shower tree is the national tree of Thailand. Its yellow flower is Thailand's national flower.

A large portrait of the king hangs outside a government building in Bangkok, which is decorated for the King's Birthday.

On the King's Birthday, buildings and homes all over Thailand are decorated with flags and portraits of the king. Around the Grand Palace and other areas of Bangkok, thousands of colorful flowers, such as marigolds, decorate the streets. There are also spectacular fireworks displays throughout the country.

(Top) A young girl in a traditional costume performs a dance in honor of the King's Birthday.

(Bottom) Fireworks are set off at *Wat Phra Kaew,* or the Temple of the Emerald Buddha. This temple is regarded as the most important temple in Thailand.

Constitution Day

King Prajadhipok

On December 10, Thai people celebrate Constitution Day, which commemorates the beginning of the Constitutional Monarchy in Thailand. Constitution Day honors the day on which Thailand's first constitution, which is the basic beliefs and laws of a country, was put into practice in 1932 by the famous King Prajadhipok.

In a Constitutional Monarchy, the king must follow the rules of the constitution. The Democracy monument in this picture celebrates Thailand's constitution.

Government offices, private buildings, and high rises are lit up with bright lights and decorated with national flags and **bunting**. There are also various royal ceremonies that take place throughout the country.

Did You Know?
Thailand's national flag is made up of five horizontal bands of red, white, and blue. The blue stripe in the middle is twice as wide as the red and white stripes. The blue stripe is believed to represent the importance of the monarchy.

Glossary

agriculture The practice of farming and raising livestock, or animals for food

ancestors People from whom other people are descended

bunting Decorations displaying the colors of a country's flag

commemorate To remember or honor

dynasty A series of rulers from the same line of descent

enlightenment Great knowledge or understanding

hymn A religious song

merit Qualities or actions that determine one's worthiness of reward or punishment

monk A member of a religious community made up of men who agree to remain poor, unmarried, and obey all the laws of their community

ordained Involved in a special ceremony to become a religious leader

processions Groups of individuals moving along in an orderly way

purify To make or become pure

retreat A time of private religious study and sacrifice

reverence The state of being revered or honored

sacred Deserving of respect or honor

scriptures The sacred writings of a religion

shrine A place or thing that is considered sacred

sins Acts that are believed to be bad

symbol Something that stands for something else

Index